HOW A LAW
IS MADE

HOW A

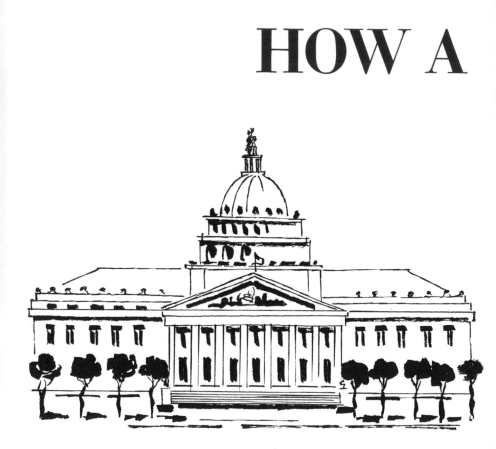

LAW IS MADE
The Story of a Bill
Against Air Pollution

by LEONARD A. STEVENS

Illustrated by ROBERT GALSTER

THOMAS Y. CROWELL COMPANY, NEW YORK

72 - 2015

By the Author:

HOW A LAW IS MADE
The Story of a Bill Against Air Pollution
NORTH ATLANTIC JET FLIGHT
THE TRUCKS THAT HAUL BY NIGHT

Manufactured in the United States of America

L.C. Card 74-101934

ISBN 0-690-40609-6

Published in Canada by Fitzhenry & Whiteside Limited, Toronto

2   3   4   5   6   7   8   9   10

ACKNOWLEDGMENTS

While this story is fiction set in a mythical state, considerable effort has been made to ensure authenticity. In that effort I had the help of many people who supplied material, granted interviews, or read the manuscript and commented upon it. I would particularly like to thank the following persons for their generous help in the preparation of this book:

The Honorable Ella T. Grasso, Secretary of the State, Connecticut.

The Honorable Arthur Tufts, President of the Senate, New Hampshire.

John Lowenthal, Professor of Law, Rutgers University.

John Lloyd Harris, three-term member of the Connecticut General Assembly, and Chairman, Republican Town Committee, Bridgewater, Connecticut.

CONTENTS

1. "There Ought to Be a Law . . ."   1
2. The Only Answer: Stop Pollution   15
3. Gathering Support for a Bill   25
4. Writing the Bill   33
5. Organizing for Action   41
6. The Committee Listens to the People   53
7. A Political Delay   71
8. Compromise and a Committee Vote   83
9. Vote, Vote, Vote   91
   Index   107

HOW A LAW
IS MADE

CHAPTER 1

"There Ought to Be a Law . . ."

One summer day in a big industrial city in a state that could have been any one of the fifty in the United States, people were deeply troubled. It was hot and humid with no sign of a breeze, and during the morning the air became heavy with smog. People's nostrils burned. Their eyes smarted and watered. Some persons coughed badly. A few older citizens, who already suffered from lung problems, had to be rushed to hospitals for treatment. Fortunately no one died, but the smog-filled day left everyone frightened. As a thundershower with a lot of wind cleared the air that evening, thousands of citizens were demanding that city and state officials make sure that there be no more such days. The people wanted a law to stop air pollution.

1

Their demands did lead to a new air-pollution law, but it was a couple of years in the making. This is the story of how it happened.

For a long time before that bad summer day people had heard a lot about air pollution, but not much had been done about it. With more and more industries, automobiles, incinerators, and jet airplanes filling the atmosphere with smog, air pollution was unquestionably increasing. But the problem appeared to be a severe health hazard only in states with huge cities like Los Angeles or New York.

The lack of immediate concern continued even when one of the state's leading doctors announced that many of his patients were suffering from lung problems that he feared were caused by air pollution. He recommended that the State Health Department make some tests around the state to check on the amount of pollution, but no one in an official position took action, and nothing came from the doctor's suggestion.

Then that frightening summer day in the large city suddenly made air pollution a big news story. Not only did residents of the city get excited about the need to fight bad air, but people all over the state became irate over what was happening to the air they breathed.

By letter, telephone call, telegram, and personal visit, they immediately got in touch with the state's top officials. They wanted action from the government to stop air pollution, and they asked for a law to do the job. Most of the appeals, therefore, went to the state's senators and representatives, who are elected by the voters to represent them in the government and to make the laws under which they live. These senators and representatives make up the General Assembly, or state legislature, which in this state meets once a year in a session that lasts from January to June. New laws are enacted by the General Assembly when it is in session. That is why

those who wanted air pollution controlled went to the legislators in their districts. They asked that a law be enacted promptly. Before the summer was over every state senator and representative had heard the appeal. Many had even been stopped on the streets of their hometowns by people who stressed that "there ought to be a law to stop air pollution."

The governor, the state's highest elected official, also heard from many voters. Most of his messages arrived by mail or telegraph at his office in the state capitol. Mainly people asked that he do everything possible to have a law passed to fight bad air. Because the governor is the person chiefly responsible for seeing that the state's laws work, he naturally has a lot to say about what new laws are needed. But some citizens also asked that he try using the existing state laws to prevent further pollution. They felt, for example, that certain health laws might be immediately useful in fighting the causes of bad air.

Since in these late summer days the General Assembly was not in session, the legislators could not easily act on the passage of the new law. The governor, however, was able to respond promptly to the public outcry. He ordered the State Health Department to hire special engineers to make a complete study of the problem. This, he decided, was an important first step in deciding what should be done in response to the citizens' demands.

Meanwhile a group of voters in the large industrial city held a meeting and discussed the ways that they might act against the air pollution now obviously endangering their health. They decided to form a state-wide organization called "the Citizens Committee for Clean Air." Someone suggested that the doctor who had first spoken out on the subject might be a good chairman, and everyone agreed. When he was telephoned, he accepted the job. The new committee soon decided that it would try to obtain a state law to control air pollution.

First, however, the organization raised money, for this was a job that would require a lot of public education through booklets, advertising in the press and on radio and television, and other expensive means. If thousands of people were going to press the General Assembly for a new law, they needed to know a lot about air pollution. The committee chairman went around the state, making speeches and requesting funds. Letters to wealthy people asked for large contributions. Newspaper stories were published telling of the need for funds.

Soon the Citizens Committee's receipts totaled nearly fifty thousand dollars, and the money was in part used to hire a consulting engineer who specialized in air pollution. Even though the State Health Department was making a study, the committee felt that a private survey could help prove the need for air-pollution controls. Furthermore, the engineer's advice would be helpful in the group's efforts to educate the public about pollution. In the next couple of months the engineer measured the amount of pollutants in the air around several cities suspected of having the most polluted air in the state. The results clearly showed that pollution was high enough to cause serious lung problems, especially among older people.

At about the same time as the engineer's data appeared in the newspapers, the State Health Department's study was released. It agreed with the engineer's facts and left little doubt that air pollution had become a major health hazard.

Following the report of these studies, several newspapers carried editorials urging the state government to pass laws controlling air pollution. One paper published a cartoon on its editorial page, showing a man and his wife walking along a city street dense with smog. The man was saying, "Keep coughing, dear, so I can find out where you are."

In late November two members of the General Assembly decided to cooperate in taking the first steps toward making a law that would meet the voters' demand for cleaning up the state's dirty air. One was a senator named Baldwin, the other a representative named Feron. Both were Democrats. They decided to sponsor a jointly written bill on air-pollution controls. Two or more legislators often get together in this way to prepare a single bill. If their bill was passed by the House of Representatives and the Senate, it would become the state's first air-pollution control law.

Senator Baldwin, a lawyer by profession, was from the big industrial city. He was interested in air pollution not only because of concern among his voters back home, but also because his family—his wife, four children, and elderly parents—breathed the dirty city air every day.

Representative Feron came from a small town, where the air was relatively clean and the people were little concerned about pollution. But being a scientist, he had a professional interest in the subject.

Late November seemed a good time to begin planning the bill. There might still be enough time

7

to have it ready for the opening of the next General Assembly session in January. So Senator Baldwin and Representative Feron went right to work on their proposed law.

For background information they met at the capitol with the chairman of the Citizens Committee for Clean Air, the commissioner of the State Health Department, both of the engineers who had made the studies on air pollution, the mayor of the state's biggest industrial city, and an official sent by the state's legislative commissioner. All these people, except the last, were now considered experts on air-pollution problems. The man sent by the legislative commissioner was an expert on the wording of legislative bills. The commissioner and his assistants, whose offices are in the capitol, have the duty of helping legislators to write their bills properly.

Everyone at the meeting soon agreed that Senator Baldwin and Representative Feron had chosen a difficult lawmaking job that would require much more knowledge about air pollution in the state than anyone had gathered to date. The law would affect thousands of people; therefore, a thorough understanding of the subject was required to make sure the measure would be fairly applied. Some of the state's largest industrial employers were helping to produce smog, and they might have to change their furnaces or machinery at great expense. Every automobile owner might also be forced to buy extra equipment to control exhaust fumes. The making of such requirements would have to be based on facts.

By the time the senator and the representative left the meeting, they had decided that they could not have a valid air-pollution control bill ready for the forthcoming session. The time needed to gather information would prevent it. The answer, they had concluded, was to write a different bill, one that if passed by the General Assembly, would order a thorough study of air pollution.

9

By January and the beginning of the new assembly session Senator Baldwin and Representative Feron, assisted by the legislative commissioner's office, had written a short bill entitled "The Establishment of a Clean-Air Task Force." If enacted into law, it would direct the governor to appoint a committee of over a hundred citizens to study air pollution. The law would also provide enough state funds for the task force to carry out its research.

The bill was introduced early in the new session, and at once the Citizens Committee for Clean Air began a campaign to see that the measure received prompt attention. Members from all over the state wrote to their senators and representatives urging that the General Assembly quickly pass the bill. "This is an urgent matter," said many of the letters. "Air pollution must be controlled before it endangers lives."

Because of public pressure, there was little doubt that the Clean-Air Task Force bill would be quickly passed by the General Assembly. It still, however, had to go through most of the procedures followed in the passage of any law. This state's General Assembly, as is the case in all but one of the state legislatures in the United States, has two houses, or *chambers* (Nebraska has only one). Its larger cham-

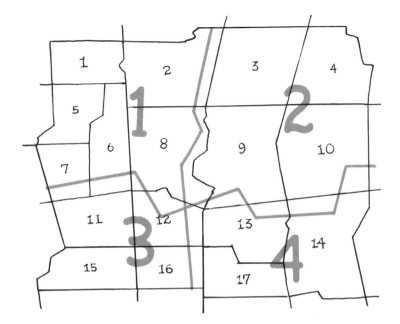

SMALL BLACK FIGURES = ASSEMBLY DISTRICTS
LARGE GRAY FIGURES = SENATORIAL DISTRICTS

ber is the House of Representatives which has, in this case, 180 members. One representative is elected from each of the 180 *assembly districts* that divide up the entire state, each district having about the same number of voters. The smaller chamber, the Senate, has forty senators. This number is determined by the division of the state into *senatorial districts,* each of which has about four times as many voters as an assembly district. As with all bills, both the House and the Senate had to vote upon and pass the Clean-Air Task Force bill to make it a law. It was given to the House of Representatives first, and within ten days the members had read the bill and voted upon it favorably. It then went to the Senate where it was also passed in a few days. The bill finally was sent to the governor who quickly signed the document, thereby making it a law.

The speed with which the bill became a law was unusual but, in this case, not surprising. Nobody opposed it, which meant that it could move very rapidly through both chambers of the General Assembly. Opposition seldom arises to a bill that requires little money and simply asks for study of a subject that voters consider important.

The new law called for the immediate establishment of the task force and the completion of its work before the next session of the General Assembly, which was now almost a year away. Within two weeks the governor had fulfilled his main obligation under the law. He had appointed 125 people to serve on the new Clean-Air Task Force, and he called the first meeting for a day in the opening week of March. At the meeting the governor gave a short speech saying that air pollution was evidently now so serious that the state government must discover ways to control it.

"We are asking that you, the Clean-Air Task Force, find a permanent program for making the air of our beautiful state clean enough to breathe without fear for our health," said the governor. "You are being asked to make this study in behalf of our legislators and the citizens of our state. It is an important service that you are about to perform."

For the remainder of the meeting the task force elected a chairman and a secretary to keep records. The new chairman, a retired businessman, thanked the group for giving him the important position, and he set the date of the next meeting for two weeks from that day.

CHAPTER 2

The Only Answer: Stop Pollution

Prior to the second meeting of the Clean-Air Task Force, the chairman spent many hours learning about the members and how best they could serve under him. They included doctors, scientists, housewives, engineers, businessmen, bankers, lawyers, college professors, and people from other professions. At the meeting the group took about two hours to decide what different areas of the subject they should study. They concluded that there were ten distinct parts to the problem, and accordingly, they helped the chairman divide the task force into ten different committees. Each committee would elect its own chairman and study one division of the subject.

One committee was to study the relationship between pure air and health. Another was to discover the amount of pollution caused by home-heating furnaces that burn oil and coal. A third was to survey the pollution caused by industry in general. One committee was to do the same for the electrical power generating industry, which burns huge quantities of oil. A financial committee was to learn the price air pollution costs each person and family in the state. Two others were to study pollution created by transportation vehicles and by incinerators and other waste-disposal equipment. A very important committee had the job of deciding how the task-force findings should be used, especially in writing a legislative bill. Last of all, a special committee had the assignment of informing people about the need for air-pollution control. Public understanding would be extremely important in gaining the support needed to get a favorable law passed in the General Assembly.

Citizens groups are at work all over the country every day, in most cases without pay, helping to solve the hundreds of problems faced by governors and legislators. Their services are extremely important but frequently unheralded. This was true of the Clean-Air Task Force. For nearly eight months the men and women on its committees worked long hours, while many of them at the same time held down regular jobs. Most of the task-force work was research conducted by the members themselves. They traveled throughout the state for a firsthand look at the causes and results of air pollution. When they encountered complicated scientific questions, the committees sought help from engineers and scientists. Some of these experts were hired; others were already available from the State Health Department. Thus the task force slowly gathered a large number of facts about air pollution.

When the research was completed, the Clean-Air Task Force chairman, who had constantly kept in touch with the studies, asked the committee chairmen to join in writing a report. The chairmen met with each other several times, and then each wrote a section of the report covering his part of the subject. The task-force chairman read and approved all the sections and then wrote both an introduction and a conclusion for them. Finally the report was printed as an attractive booklet in thousands of copies.

One day in late November the *Clean-Air Task Force Report* was officially presented to the governor, who had invited Senator Baldwin and Representative Feron to share in the occasion. Members of the press were there, and the brief ceremony was carried on radio and television. The task-force chairman made the presentation to the governor, and each man gave a short speech stressing the importance of the subject. The study, said the task-force chairman, made the urgency of air-pollution control very clear.

The *Report* received a lot of public attention in the state's newspapers because it contained some pretty startling facts. The amount of air pollution reported for communities all over the state was surprisingly high in many cases. Automobiles, said the *Report*, were pouring nearly two million tons of pollutants into the air each year. Big electrical generating plants were adding nearly a half million tons per year. Heating plants and rubbish burners were producing another quarter million tons of air pollutants.

These figures had more meaning when the *Report* explained that air pollution was costing every citi-

zen money, as well as causing the discomforts of poor health. Bad air was damaging crops and cutting farm income. It was forcing families to spend more on housecleaning. Paint on outside walls was not lasting as long as it should. But most serious of all were added doctors' bills, most evident when the task force had studied the lung disease *emphysema,* which is suffered mostly by older people. In the past ten years the disease's rate had increased nearly three times in the state. When the researchers totaled the costs of such problems, they discovered that the average family was now forced to spend six hundred dollars a year because of air pollution.

"But the family cost of air pollution given in this study," said the *Report,* "does not cover all the damage resulting from bad air. For example, we can be fairly certain but can not prove that many deaths occur sooner than they would if we all were able to breathe clean air. It is impossible to cover

the full meaning of such conclusions. But we can definitely say that life in our state is not as comfortable as it would be if the air were kept clean. This is something that you can not measure in dollars."

At the end of the *Report* the Clean-Air Task Force chairman wrote: "There is no substitute for air. Man must have it in large quantities. It must be instantly available, any time, everywhere. It must be pure, and there is only one way to keep it so: STOP POLLUTION!"

This plea was then followed by two lists of recommendations. One was for the governor, and one was for the General Assembly.

The governor's list suggested things to do that were already within his power. For example, the task force recommended that he order the State Health Department to build monitoring stations around the state to test the air night and day and to sound a warning whenever pollution became critically dangerous. These stations could also test pollution control once it was established.

The recommendations for the General Assembly contained what the task force would like to see enacted into state law. The first and most important recommendations called for a ten-member

"Clean-Air Commission" which would have the power to control air pollution. If the commission's orders were disobeyed, the task force recommended a fine of up to five thousand dollars a week—an amount obviously aimed at large industrial offenders.

The *Task Force Report* also called for outlawing the use of certain kinds of oil for home heating and electrical generating plants. Owners, it said, should be given two years to change their furnaces and machinery so that they could use fuel that produces comparatively little air pollution. The proposed law would also force trucks and automobiles to carry pollution-prevention devices for their exhausts. New motor vehicles, said the *Report*, should not be sold without these devices, and used-car owners should be given six months to have them installed.

While the *Task Force Report* increased favorable publicity for pollution control, it awakened some opposition—though not in the public view. The chairman of the State Manufacturers Association wrote a letter to the governor contesting some of the *Report's* recommendations. He stated that he was not against a clean-air program, but he did feel that the task force's ideas would be unfair to the big industries. Outlawing certain fuel oils, he said, would cost manufacturers millions of dollars. Their huge furnaces would have to be converted to burn different oil. The pollution-free fuels would also cost more per gallon and add up to millions of extra dollars per year. The association's chairman said that existing furnaces could be equipped with purification devices that would remove pollutants despite the kind of oil burned. This way of attacking pollution, he argued, would be much fairer to the industries concerned.

The governor asked the task-force chairman to help him answer the letter. The reply said that the task force's study committee on industry had concluded that although purification equipment helps, it is not really satisfactory. "It can present a serious problem created by a constant need for expert adjustment," the governor wrote. "An engineer sometimes has to regulate purification devices continually to keep them working efficiently. It's a matter of opinion, but the Clean-Air Task Force has concluded that the only certain control for this kind of pollution is to change to a different kind of oil."

Other than this minor debate by mail there was little if any opposition to the *Task Force Report*. However, those pollution-control supporters who were experienced in promoting public issues wished this was not the case. They would have preferred more public argument on at least some part of the study. A little verbal heat creates interest, which in turn can help educate the public on a subject. But no one seemed willing to fight the *Report* openly.

"After all," said the chairman, "who can come out against clean air?"

CHAPTER 3

Gathering Support for a Bill

Before the task-force study was published, Senator Baldwin and Representative Feron had gone to the capitol to talk about their plans to introduce an air-pollution control bill at the next session of the General Assembly. It was between sessions when the assembly is represented by a Legislative Council, thirty senators and representatives chosen to conduct the legislature's routine business (but not to pass laws). Decisions have constantly to be made for such a large, important organization as the General Assembly, whether or not it is in session. Plans have to be laid for its next sitting, especially regarding the priority of considering the various bills to be introduced. In November at one of the council's weekly meetings Senator Baldwin and

25

Representative Feron paid the Legislative Council a visit.

Both men pointed out that they were still anxious for a good air-pollution bill to come before the next General Assembly session. They reported on the progress of the Clean-Air Task Force and explained that its forthcoming report would contain the facts and recommendations needed for the next important step, writing the air-pollution control bill itself. After a short discussion, the council agreed that the voters wanted controls and that no time should be wasted in placing a bill before the General Assembly.

"Since you gentlemen were the authors of the Clean-Air Task Force legislation," said the council's chairman, "we are, of course, expecting you to prepare a pollution control bill. People are looking to you for leadership on the subject. I can assure you that we will give your bill priority for consideration at the next session."

Soon after they met with the Legislative Council, the two legislators paid another important visit. Seeking more support for their effort, they went to the state Democratic Central Committee headquarters with offices in the capital city. This state's central committee consists of eighty leading Democrats from all over the state. They are elected by their party for a two-year term. The members themselves elect their own leader, the Democratic state chairman. The same is true for the Republican party. The two parties' central committees are the most powerful political groups in the state. When they call upon the legislators of their party to unite for or against the passage of a bill, it may well decide the fate of the measure. This was on the minds of Senator Baldwin and Representative Feron when they made an appointment with the Democratic state chairman.

As the visit began, the chairman talked in a philosophical vein for several moments. He explained that his job was like a balancing act. On the one hand, he had to see that his party supported good legislation needed by the people. Because of such support the people would be inclined to give their votes to Democratic candidates. On the other hand, to gain political support is very much a matter of timing. A good move made at the wrong time can fail. Or if you neglect making the move at the right time, it may never be possible to succeed with it later. Then party candidates suffer at election time.

"Have you thought about timing?" asked the chairman, who had his party's platform in mind.

The platform is simply a guiding statement of what a party stands for, and in this state a new one is adopted every two years by delegates from across the state meeting in party convention.

"Usually we have time to consider and support such matters as air-pollution control through the platform," continued the chairman. "Compared to most legislative efforts, your proposed bill seems to be moving very quickly. Last year when our current platform was adopted at the state convention, your task force hadn't even been thought of. Now before our next convention in May you are proposing to go before the General Assembly with a bill."

"The right timing," said Senator Baldwin, "is precisely why we are in such a hurry. People are stirred up. They want action."

"Well, now, are you really sure of that?" said the chairman. "The Citizens Committee for Clean Air has been making a lot of noise, but I wonder if people have actually been paying that much attention. We have to be realistic."

"I don't think there is any question about it," said Representative Feron. "I am firmly convinced that the Citizens Committee is bringing the public effectively behind a widespread demand for air-pollution control. And don't think for a minute that

the committee doesn't have the politicians in mind."

"You say that we have nothing in our platform about air-pollution control," said Senator Baldwin to the party chairman, "but I can assure you that the Citizens Committee for Clean Air won't agree. They are not going to let us forget what the platform says about public health in general. The Democratic party pledged itself to take leadership in any fight for the protection of public health against any force that might endanger it. You know the statement. It's on page 22 of the platform booklet. I have already been told that the air-pollution control leaders have read that page and just assume we mean that we will fight for clean air."

"Okay, they've got an argument, no doubt about it," said the chairman. "But again may I be a little realistic? I wonder, for instance, if the Citizens Committee really has the ear of our factory workers. They add up to a lot of Democratic voters. I would hate to wake up some morning and find that someone had talked the workingman into fearing air-pollution control. It is conceivable that the fear of losing one's job could be stirred up in relation to such control."

"On the other hand, the workingmen had better be very concerned about pollution," said Representative Feron. "Most of their families live in our big industrial cities where the problem has been talked about continually. That's where bad air is hurting people's health the most."

"But don't forget," replied the party chairman, "most of our labor voters work right in the factories where the owners are likely to oppose your air-pollution bill. Are they going to frighten their employees by saying that pollution control can affect their jobs?"

"I don't see how they could prove anything of the kind," said the senator. "Anyhow we are not sure that industry will oppose the bill to that extent."

"Maybe not, but I don't want to take any

chances," said the chairman. "There are a lot of other big problems in this state besides air pollution, and some of them depend very much on our holding every vote possible for the Democratic party."

"But don't forget the political power of the Citizens Committee for Clean Air," said Representative Feron. "Look at the membership, and you will even see a large number of labor leaders. If we don't get behind a good air-pollution control bill this year, I know the Democratic party won't be allowed to forget what we have failed to do."

"I am sure we will get behind the bill," said the chairman, "but first let me talk to a few of our friends in labor. Let's be sure of their reaction before we make any final decision. Meanwhile what about the Republicans? Any idea of what they are going to do?"

"That puzzles me," said the representative. "In the House I find Republicans saying they favor action, but they are not as enthusiastic as the Democrats. They may have some power-company problems, and you know why."

The state chairman understood. He was aware that the Republican state chairman had once been the vice-president of a large electrical power company. Most of the man's close friends were still in the company, and they might ask him not to support a bill on air pollution.

Although Senator Baldwin and Representative Feron hoped to have Republican support for their proposed legislation, they knew it wasn't absolutely necessary to the bill's passage. The General Assembly was now controlled by the Democrats. In the House, 108 of the 180 members (60 percent) were Democrats. In the Senate they held 22 of the 40 seats (55 percent), which was a narrow margin. But if all the Democrats in both the Senate and House stuck together, they could pass any bill desired because they held a voting majority.

"I think that you gentlemen can feel sure of our full party support on your bill," said the state chairman. "I will talk with some labor people this week. I also want to talk the matter over with the state central committee next Monday when we meet. I will telephone you a day or so after the meeting."

CHAPTER 4

Writing the Bill

While most people were busy with the Christmas season, Senator Baldwin and Representative Feron spent much of their time writing an air-pollution control bill. On December tenth they received a call from the Democratic state chairman who reported that his labor friends and the party's state central committee were ready to support action on air pollution. Encouraged, the two legislators went to the legislative commissioner's office where a lawyer was assigned to help them put their recommendations into language that could become law if enacted by the General Assembly.

Before writing a word, however, the legislators and their lawyer assistant made sure that the bill would not be at cross-purposes with existing laws.

Above all, it would have to be *constitutional,* so as not to conflict with the constitutions of this state and the United States. Both constitutions, which are similar, protect the most basic rights of individuals, and air-pollution control might very well interfere with some of these rights.

People, for example, have always been free to do pretty much as they choose around their own homes and property. But here was a law that might force citizens to give up some of these freedoms for the good of everyone. It might state that they could not use certain kinds of fuels in furnaces or that they were not to burn leaves in their yards. Would such restrictions be constitutional? The lawmakers

thought they would be, but actually they might never be sure unless a violator of such a law was taken to court and the judges of the land, perhaps even the Supreme Court of the United States, decided the question. If declared *unconstitutional*, the legislation would, of course, be useless because it couldn't be enforced. Such a fate was to be avoided while writing the bill.

The senator and representative with their assistant also had to ensure that their proposed law would not conflict with any already on the books. This required a careful search of hundreds of existing state laws. To his surprise the lawyer found one nearly seventy-five years old that might cause trouble. In one of the state's small industrial towns a glue factory using raw material distilled from animal bones had dumped its extremely bad-smelling waste in an open field. Complaints about the odor got nowhere until several people spoke to their state representative who arranged for the General Assembly to enact a law forcing such factories to burn the waste. When the law, still in force, was pointed out to Senator Baldwin, he telephoned the town and found the factory had closed twenty years ago. Furthermore, it had been the only one of its kind in the state. But while the law now seemed to have no valid application, some observant lawyer might use it to protect a client who was burning waste in violation of the new air-pollution law. The legislators therefore decided to write a paragraph into their bill automatically repealing the old law if the new one passed.

By New Year's Day the writing of the bill was completed in several pages of very carefully worded language. It was entitled, "An Act Concerning the Elimination of Air Pollution." It carried a simple statement of purpose which said, "To provide for control of pollution of the air of the State." The written matter began, as all bills begin, "Be it enacted by the Senate and House of Representatives in General Assembly convened . . ."; and then it continued, paragraph after paragraph.

In the first of its twenty-eight numbered sections the bill defined what the law would mean by *air pollution*. The definition called it "the presence in the outdoor atmosphere of one or more pollutants injurious to the public welfare." Such air pollution, continued the bill, would (1) injure the health of human, animal, or plant life, (2) damage property, or (3) interfere with a person's enjoyment of his life and property. It is important that a law define exactly what it is for or against. This can become extremely important to lawyers and judges trying to apply the measure in the way that the General Assembly intended.

The next several sections of the bill were the most important. They began by simply stating, "There shall be a clean air commission of ten members appointed by the governor." The bill then explained that all ten must be registered voters but that none could be employed by the state. One member must be a doctor and one an engineer with knowledge of air-pollution control. Two other commissioners would, in a sense, represent business to ensure the fair treatment of companies on which pollution controls might be forced: one was to be employed by a manufacturing industry and the other by an electrical generating company. The bill said the remaining six commissioners should be chosen from other walks of life best representing the general public.

The measure next explained the commission's rights, which would make it a very powerful organization. First it could write and enforce state regulations to control air pollution. For enforcement, it could inspect public buildings or any machinery suspected of producing air pollution. It could hire experts to decide on the cause of and the people responsible for air pollution. The commission could then order offenders to stop polluting the air. If disobeyed, it could bring a violator into court where a judge might fine him as much as five thousand dollars a week until he corrected the source of the pollution.

When people were forced to install expensive air-pollution control equipment, the law would help them out by reducing their state taxes somewhat. In cases where towns burned garbage in dumps that pollute the air, the commission would have the right to grant state loans to help the communities buy incinerators to prevent such pollution.

The new law would allow other state commissions to join forces with the Clean Air Commission to stop air pollution. By cooperating with the Motor Vehicle Commission, the Clean Air Commission might force a car owner either to install a device to stop exhaust fumes or have his automobile license taken away from him.

Finally the law would provide nearly a quarter million dollars a year for use in any way the new commission decided suitable for the control of air pollution. Most of the money would pay for offices and a staff to help the commissioners.

Anyone reading the full bill could understand it

was an important and powerful piece of legislation, truly a document of the late twentieth century. While science and engineering were producing miracles, they were also seriously interfering with Nature's miracles, especially the air and water that sustain all life. Men were finally doing something about it by law. The new bill on air pollution was an important part of the effort.

CHAPTER 5

Organizing for Action

On January seventh, the first day of the new General Assembly session, it seemed that everybody in the state was at the capitol. The halls inside the old granite building were packed with people, and the noise they made resounded from the marble floors, stairways, and columns. In addition to the 40 senators and 180 representatives, there were dozens of clerks, messengers, and secretaries milling about the halls of the capitol. A dozen or more uniformed guards tried to keep visitors in the open public passageways, so they wouldn't disturb the nearby offices where important people, like the governor, were at work. Newspapers had sent reporters and photographers who were looking for stories and pictures of important political figures. Many

41

lobbyists, as such people are called, were roaming through the halls. Lobbyists work for businesses, labor unions, clubs, and other organizations, and they were here to try to influence lawmaking in favor of those for whom they were lobbying. The hallways were also crowded with citizens from every walk of life. Some had come to talk with their senators and representatives about new laws; others were simply interested in observing their elected representatives at work on the first day of the new legislative session. No one could witness the scene that day without realizing that lawmaking is a very public business.

Both the Senate and the House of Representatives were called into session at the designated hour of ten in the morning. Each body met in a large oak-paneled auditorium where the legislators sat at desks much like those that were once found in most schoolrooms. In each chamber there was a podium (at the front of the desks). Up and around three sides of both rooms were galleries where several hundred visitors might sit to observe the proceedings. In both auditoriums the Republican legislators sat together on the right, the Democrats on the left. All the members of both the Senate and the House knew one another. Everyone had served in the

General Assembly for at least one year of a two-year term, and many had been there for several terms. It was something like the first day of school with old friends greeting one another.

After a prayer and taking their oaths of office as a body, the legislators started organizing the General Assembly. Mainly this meant choosing and administering oaths to the leaders and clerks for the new session. The most important offices were filled by the Democrats, because they had the majority of votes in each chamber. This made them the "controlling" party and thereby able to elect the most important leaders from their own ranks.

In the House the top position is that of "the Speaker" who stands at the podium at the front and conducts the business of the House of Representatives. The same duty in the Senate is more or less shared by two men. The top Senate leader is the state's lieutenant governor, who is elected by the people and serves in the role of vice-president prepared to take over the governor's job should he die or leave office for some reason. The lieutenant governor is also the president of the Senate, and he presides over the Senate as the Speaker does over the House. But when the lieutenant governor can't be present, the Senate's business is conducted by the president pro tempore, a senator elected to the position at the opening of each session.

On the first day members in both the Senate and the House elected a majority leader, minority leader, and assistants for each chamber. The first was chosen from the Democrats, the majority party, while the second came from the Republicans, the minority party. These men would lead the General Assembly members of their respective parties and attempt to have them work and vote together in translating the parties' political philosophies and purposes into legislation.

When the job of organizing the House was complete, the new Speaker began the traditional ceremony of inviting the Senate to sit with the House. He appointed a small committee of representatives who walked in a group around the building to the

Senate chamber where they announced that their colleagues were organized and waiting for the senators to attend a joint session to hear the governor give a welcoming speech.

Shortly the 40 senators led by the lieutenant governor filed into the House and sat down with the 180 representatives. Since the lieutenant governor was now the highest official present, he went to the podium and opened the joint session, calling on the newly elected chaplain of the Senate for a prayer. The lieutenant governor then appointed a committee of senators and representatives and sent them to invite the governor to come from his office and address the joint session. The committee soon returned with their honored guest. As they entered the House, there was applause from the 220 legislators and the visitors in the galleries.

When the auditorium was quiet, the governor began his speech, reviewing in twenty-five minutes the most important matters before the state government. At the same time he recommended legislative action to meet some of the state's most serious problems. He spoke of the need for finding new ways for raising money through taxes. He said that the rising rate of crime in the state might be stopped if the General Assembly would strengthen some old laws and consider some new ones. He talked about the ever-increasing costs of education and stressed that the legislators should consider giving more financial assistance to help towns and cities pay for schools.

In the middle of his speech the governor began a discussion of the state's natural resources by calling for a law to control air pollution. He reminded his listeners that the past two sessions of the General Assembly had enacted laws to clean up the state's polluted water supplies.

"Now it is even more important," said the governor, "to turn immediately to another, perhaps more serious, kind of pollution. It has been clearly demonstrated by scientific tests that the very breath of life for nearly every citizen in our state has been seriously dirtied. This costly pollution damages our health. It leads to discomforts that cut into the pleasures of living, especially for the many elderly people who have reached the years when they should be able to enjoy life. Air pollution can not be allowed to remain in this state one hour longer than necessary. Therefore, I call upon the General Assembly to consider this matter as promptly as possible and to take the legislative steps necessary to combat air pollution at its sources."

The statement was received by a loud ovation from legislators and spectators. The Citizens Committee for Clean Air had asked a large number of its members to be in the galleries when the governor made his expected remarks on air pollution. Their brief but resounding effort was worth the long automobile rides many had taken to the state capitol that morning. It alerted the full General Assembly to the fact that the voters wanted action on air pollution. The visitors again showed their enthusiasm by cheering and clapping when the governor finished his address.

The following day the Senate and House met to organize the *standing committees,* which are automatically formed with each new session. These committees study particular kinds of legislative work certain to need attention year after year, such as roads, prisons, labor, education, and fish and game. Some of the General Assembly's twenty-eight standing committees have remained in force half a century or more. They are the legislature's work brigades. All the bills introduced in a session are divided up among the committees for study, discussion, public hearings, and finally, voting to recommend whether the assembly as a whole should pass or reject each measure. In point of fact, the standing committees do most of the legislature's decision-making because the Senate and House follow the committees' recommendations for all but a few bills.

In the General Assembly of our story these committees are organized *jointly*. This means that each one of them serves both chambers and contains members from both the Senate and the House of Representatives. Actually most state legislatures do not use *joint committees*. Instead they have two committees, one in the Senate and one in the House, working on each subject category. But this causes much of the committee work to be done twice, so many political scientists think that joint committees are more efficient.

In the Senate of our story, committee assignments are made by the president pro tempore, and in the House by the Speaker. Their selections of committee members are usually guided by the political parties. Actually the decisions of who will serve on what committee are generally made in advance of the session in private meetings called *party caucuses*. Each caucus is attended by the legislators of only one political party, along with party officials such as the state chairman. At these meetings the Democrats decide who from their ranks should serve on what committees, and the same is true of Republican caucuses. The controlling political party, however, has the chance to pick the majority of members, for each committee keeps a balance in the number of Democrats and Republicans comparable to that held in the General Assembly itself.

In party caucuses, which are actually used for many purposes before and during a session of the General Assembly, a political party exerts a powerful influence over lawmaking. While a party's state chairman may not be an elected member of the Assembly, through the caucuses he may have more influence than even a legislator in a top position. Here he can mold opinion and then unite his party members behind measures in the various joint committees and on the floor of the Senate and the House. If he is chairman of the majority party in the General Assembly, his power, of course, is even greater.

Because of what the air-pollution bill involved, it would be placed before the joint Committee on Public Health and Safety. When the committee's composition had been discussed in a Democratic caucus the week before the General Assembly opened, the Democratic state chairman revealed that a request had been made of him by the Citizens Committee for Clean Air. The citizens' group had noted that if custom was followed and all the committee members of the previous session were retained on the Committee on Public Health and Safety, the Democrats would still have two vacancies to fill. Two previous committee members from the party had left the General Assembly to accept important jobs in the State Health Department.

"Now here is what the Citizens Committee is proposing," the state chairman had said in the caucus, "and frankly I think it is a bad suggestion. They want to see the two openings filled by Senator Baldwin and Representative Feron."

"I would like to decline being on the committee," Senator Baldwin responded quickly. "I am deeply concerned with air pollution because of the way it is affecting my people back home. But I am not otherwise well acquainted with matters of public health and safety. The Committee on Public Health and Safety takes up bills on many matters besides air pollution. I am a lawyer, as you know, and can serve much better right on the Judiciary Committee where I have been in past sessions."

"I am glad that you are declining," the state chairman said. "To put both sponsors of the air-pollution bill on the committee would give a bad look to it. It would seem as if we were trying to rig the committee for the sake of this bill only. I shall write the Citizens Committee and tell them that you refuse the position anyhow. Now how about you, Mr. Feron? We could put you on Public Health and Safety in one of the two openings."

"You know, sir, I would like to be on it," Representative Feron answered, "but not if putting me there would look as though the only reason we were doing it was to obtain a vote for our bill. My background in science, however, might be useful to the committee on many matters in the future."

"Appointing you is not much of a risk to run," the state chairman said. "You might have gone on the committee anyhow. You have the background. But let's say it does enhance your own bill. Is that bad? It's a good bill. If I have agreement here in the caucus, I'm for putting you on the committee."

No one disagreed with the assignment, and Representative Feron had thus been listed for one of the two open positions. The other was filled by a new representative, a retired doctor, who had been recommended by several legislators.

On the second day of the new session the selections of the party caucuses for committee members were made official in the Senate by the president pro tempore and in the House by the Speaker. Both stood before their respective chambers and rapidly read off the lists of assignments for the twenty-eight standing committees. While the uninformed observer might think these two gentlemen had stayed up all night sorting out who was to serve on what committee, the informed onlooker knew that the choices had actually been settled the week before in party caucuses.

When the assignments were completed, the General Assembly was ready for the day-by-day work of the new session. The legislators could now turn to their business of making laws.

CHAPTER 6

The Committee Listens to the People

The air-pollution control measure prepared by Senator Baldwin and Representative Feron was among the first of the nearly fifteen hundred bills submitted to the new session of the General Assembly. Every bill has to start its legislative career in either the Senate or the House. The two legislators had decided that their bill should be a *House bill,* which meant that Representative Feron would introduce it.

On the third morning of the session he took the bill, typewritten on a special form, to the clerk of the House who assigned it the number 1022. The clerk then sent the bill to the Speaker of the House for the first of three *readings.* The method of presenting a bill is still described in terminology re-

53

tained from past centuries when many English law-makers did not know how to read, and each measure was read aloud three times to ensure that it was understood. Of course, the modern legislator can read, but our lawmaking procedure still calls for a bill to be presented—usually in written form—three times to a legislative body before a vote is taken. The first reading of Bill 1022 simply consisted of its number and title being announced to the House by the clerk at the request of the Speaker, who also stated that he was assigning the measure to the joint Public Health and Safety Committee.

With these formalities over, Bill 1022 was on its way through the legislative mill. Copies were sent to the Senate for introduction by the president pro tempore. And copies were also sent to the Public

Health and Safety Committee. After the committee studied the bill and made a recommendation for or against it, the measure would be sent back to the House for its second and third readings.

For the next few weeks little happened on Bill 1022 because legislators were busy studying the growing mass of proposed laws being submitted within the three-week period allowed at a session's beginning for the introduction of new measures. However, the Citizens Committee for Clean Air was making sure that no legislator would overlook the fact that an air-pollution bill was before the General Assembly. As soon as 1022 was introduced, the citizen group went into action with a state-wide program to support the measure. The organization's letter-writing committee was soon calling on people to write their senators and representatives asking for an air-pollution control law.

In addition, the Citizens Committee had a special program aimed at all twenty-four members of the Public Health and Safety Committee. In their home districts intensive campaigns were underway to stir up interest in 1022. Every day, for example, housewives were holding educational coffee hours to discuss the bill. A woman might invite a dozen neighbors to a session in her home, at the conclu-

55

sion of which she would urge that everyone write or telephone his state senator and representative requesting that 1022 receive prompt, favorable action. It resulted in committee members receiving boxes of mail every day. When the legislators went home at night or over the weekend, people would telephone them or stop them in the street to proclaim that air-pollution control was needed.

Legislators all over the country are familiar with such public pressure, and they have to judge it along with the bills involved. Sometimes a small number of people can stir up a surprising amount of mail or telephone calls for or against a bill, yet the effort may really not represent true public feeling. If all the messages say exactly the same thing, it is likely that they have been prompted by a comparatively small pressure group, and that the senders have probably not given the subject much thought. A legislator who follows this kind of pressure may find himself voting for a bad bill or against a good one. On the other hand, he can't ignore messages composed with thought and originality. They may very well demonstrate that people are truly and deeply concerned. In most instances, this was the kind of letter coming from the Citizens Committee's efforts.

The first formal action on 1022 occurred in February when the Public Health and Safety Committee set a date for a public hearing, a formal occasion at which anyone could speak for or against the bill. Major bills under this General Assembly's rules are subject to hearings, but many receive little or no public attention. When a bill catches a lot of interest, however, the hearing may draw a huge crowd from all over the state. Some of the people come to speak in favor of the bill; some like parts of it but want changes made; others completely oppose it; but the largest number come to listen because they are interested in seeing the bill either passed or rejected. Bill 1022 was certain to draw a crowd, for the work of the Citizens Committee on Clean Air ensured the presence of several hundred people who were supporting it. Of course, there might also be those who were against it, but as the hearing date was set, no one knew for sure who the opposition would be.

By a quarter of ten on the morning of the hearing day large numbers of visitors were arriving at the state capitol, and guards were directing them to a third-floor auditorium where TV cameras and lights had been set up. The majority of them had come at the urging of the Citizens Committee for Clean Air,

but other interests related to air pollution were also
represented. Several lobbyists were there in behalf
of industrial organizations, one of these being the
State Manufacturers Association and another a
council supported by the state's petroleum companies. Several civic organizations were represented. A woman from the State Public Health Association and another from the League of Women
Voters intended to speak. And there were a half-
dozen state officials, the most important of whom
was the commissioner who directed the Health Department. Those who wanted to address the joint
committee were asked to write down their names on
a pad of paper by the door.

At ten o'clock, seventeen of the twenty-six members of the Public Health and Safety Committee filed into the crowded auditorium and took their seats behind a long table at the front of the room. Representative Feron was among them. The committee's chairman, a senator, rapped a gavel, requested that the room quiet down, and then asked if there was anyone who wished to speak who had not listed his name on the pad of paper that he now held in his hand. When no one responded, the chairman made a short statement about the purpose of the hearing, and then he called out the first name signed on the list.

It was the lobbyist from the State Manufacturers Association. He walked quickly down an aisle to one of the two podiums set up with microphones and immediately started reading aloud from a typewritten statement. First he said that the businessmen of the state were all for clean air. They recognized that pollution was growing increasingly serious, but then he added that they felt the problem was not yet as drastic as some people believed.

With this the supporters of air-pollution control suddenly became restless, and some started talking to each other. The chairman rapped his gavel and asked for silence so the testimony could continue.

The disturbance led the TV cameramen to turn on their lights and train their lenses on this speaker who was obviously controversial.

The lobbyist continued by saying that many of the state manufacturers believed that Bill 1022 would be unfair if it were passed in its present form —at least, this year. He said the businessmen felt that if given a chance, they could prevent a lot of industrial pollution without a law. He was, in other words, calling for self-control by the industries themselves.

"At least, we should be given an opportunity to do something about pollution control on our own," said the lobbyist. "If industry has done nothing about the problem in a couple of years, then it might be fair to pass a control law."

"Why haven't you already done something?" said a man in a loud voice in the middle of the audience.

The chairman banged his gavel hard. "Please do not speak unless you are recognized by the chair," he stated loudly. "We are here to listen to everyone who has anything to say on this bill, but the hearing must be orderly."

The lobbyist, having nothing more to say, returned to his seat. The room's noise level increased, and the chairman's gavel was heard again. The supporters of Bill 1022 were obviously surprised and shaken. The TV cameras and lights swung toward the audience to catch the look of concern on people's faces. For months members of the Citizens Committee for Clean Air had only heard comments favorable to their cause. For the first time many realized that their favorite bill might not necessarily pass without opposition. It was an unpleasant surprise that often comes to those inexperienced in the ways of public debate.

The committee chairman called the second speaker, another lobbyist who represented the state's petroleum companies. The lobbyists, unlike the inexperienced people who desired to speak, had realized from past hearings that they would have to sign up to testify, so they had arrived early and put their names at the top of the list. This second speaker, repeating what the first had said, began by declaring, "Yes, we agree that the control of air pollution is important, but we also ask, Why the great hurry? Given a chance, we can do what the bill requests without the passage of a law."

He then led into an attack on a specific section of the bill, one providing that violators could be fined up to five thousand dollars a week.

"This bill as now written does not clearly define

what it is that makes a person a violator," stated the lobbyist. "As we read it, the proposed law would make it possible to fine a man for burning wastepaper in his backyard incinerator. Could you seriously consider making it possible to fine such a person five thousand dollars a week?"

When the speaker finished, Representative Feron requested and was granted the chance to speak by the committee chairman. He asked the lobbyist: "Do you understand that such a fine would be strictly up to the Clean Air Commission? Do you believe that to fine a man five thousand dollars a week for burning trash would be a judicious move from a commission that we assume will consist of reasonable people? That certainly is not the intent of the law proposed. If you read it again, you may realize that the intent is to use the largest possible fines only when necessary and only against major violators who have that kind of money."

"We don't interpret it that way," said the lobbyist, and he sat down abruptly.

The pollution-control supporters in the audience began to clap for Representative Feron, but they were stopped fast with a sharp bang of the gavel and the chairman's saying, "Quiet, please!"

The third speaker changed the entire tone of the

meeting. He was the commissioner of the State Health Department, and he read a carefully written statement based very much on the *Clean-Air Task Force Report.*

He was followed by the doctor who was the chairman of the Citizens Committee for Clean Air who had a prepared statement but hardly read a paragraph from it. Instead, he gave an impromptu answer to the two lobbyists who had begun the testimony. He argued that the problem had grown far too big for self-control to be effective. He also said that if self-control had any merit it would have already been applied around the state with far greater benefit than was now evident. He had no knowledge that there had been any such application.

The hearing continued until nearly two o'clock in the afternoon with most of the speakers favorable to the passage of Bill 1022. One man, however, offered a criticism which everyone agreed needed serious consideration. He was an official of the State Firemen's Association who was an expert in the training of fire fighters. He pointed out that one section of the proposed legislation could seriously hinder the training of firemen.

"In order to learn how to fight fires of all kinds,"

he explained, "we have to burn various materials and chemicals in open fires. As we understand this bill, it would make some of our most important training programs illegal. If we are to train firemen effectively, we must provide firsthand experience with open fires of all kinds. We therefore respectfully suggest that Bill 1022 be revised to make an exception for such training. It might give our training directors the opportunity to obtain special permits from the proposed air-pollution control commission."

The chairman of the Public Health and Safety Committee made a note about this request and thanked the fireman for his remarks.

Next on the speakers' list was a college student

with an interesting suggestion. He pointed out that students, having little knowledge of air pollution, seldom realized that important, interesting careers exist in this field for engineers. The young man urged that Bill 1022 include a section on scholarships that would encourage students to specialize in air-pollution control. Scholarships might offer financial help from state funds to be issued to worthy students by the proposed Clean Air Commission. The chairman of the committee, obviously attracted to the idea, commended the young man for offering the suggestion.

One of the last speakers was the vice-president of a major electrical power company. As with the others who had already spoken unfavorably of 1022, this official spent a couple of minutes supporting the aims of the task force and agreeing with the need for air-pollution control. But he was concerned with the amount of time that the law would give his company to make the technical changes needed to prevent pollution. Two years was not enough; five years would be much fairer, he maintained. With great courtesy and respect he specifically asked that the committee change the bill accordingly. The chairman thanked the vice-president for coming and assured him that the change would be considered.

But the company official had chosen a poor time to make his statement, for he was followed by a person whose emotional appeal gained a great deal of sympathy for the cause of air-pollution control. He was an elderly gentleman who represented a large senior citizens' club located in the industrial city where pollution had reached dangerous levels two summers earlier. His voice was weak and hoarse, and he excused himself for having difficulty in talking. Everyone in the room was exceptionally quiet as the aged man said that he was one of sixteen persons in his club who suffered from emphysema. They did not necessarily blame the disease on air pollution, but they were aware that bad air could be a cause and continuing source of discomfort. His fellow members had elected him to attend the hearings and speak out in favor of Bill 1022.

The elderly citizen with the scratchy voice made some of the committee members nervous; they wondered if he wasn't using his illness to unfair advantage. But without question, his was the most effective testimony in the entire hearing. The TV cameras and microphones focused on him to catch every word. The press, radio, and TV representatives, with their sense for the dramatic, recognized the old man's human interest value.

The few remaining speakers were comparatively routine, and they all favored the proposed law. When everyone who was to testify had spoken, the chairman adjourned the hearing. It was given several minutes on television news that evening, and the elderly speaker was the star performer. Those who had struggled to put across such legislation for months had never seen nor heard of the man before, but he had suddenly become a prime mover of their cause.

**WHEN STATE LAW
IS NEEDED**

1

**THE PEOPLE
DEMAND IT**

2

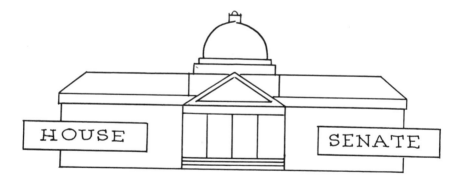

GENERAL ASSEMBLY MAKES IT

3

GOVERNOR AND
STATE DEPARTMENTS
APPLY AND ENFORCE IT

4

COURTS
MAKE SURE IT
IS FAIR

5

THE PEOPLE BENEFIT FROM IT

6

CHAPTER 7

A Political Delay

The hearing ensured that "the voice of the people" had been officially solicited and heard. The legislators might now receive many private communications about 1022—letters, phone calls, and visits—but the Committee on Public Health and Safety had exercised the democratic act of listening to all comers. The committee's decision on Bill 1022 would now turn largely on discussion in *executive session*, which meant meeting in private.

The first such discussion on the committee's agenda was scheduled for March 5. Only eighteen of the members were present but that made a quorum, which meant that enough members were present for a vote in case one was taken on 1022 that day. The group consisted of two women, both from the House, and sixteen men from the House and Senate, many of whom were smoking cigars and clouding the small meeting room with smoke.

"Mr. Feron," said the committee chairman, "this is pretty much your bill. It's only fair, I guess, to give you the first word."

Representative Feron coughed and then laughed as he said, "If we don't vote immediately in favor of the bill, the air pollution in here will keep us from ever getting to it."

The two women clapped and glowered at the cigar smokers, who smiled but continued puffing. One of the men said, "Cigar smoke is part of politics. As Harry Truman said, 'If you can't stand the smoke, you should get out of the kitchen.'"

"You mean the heat, not the smoke," said one of the ladies, correcting the attempt to quote President Truman.

"Same difference," said the cigar smoker.

This exchange made a point and also helped start the meeting off with good feelings. Representative Feron then offered a short, serious plea for the committee to give Bill 1022 a *joint favorable*. This would mean that the joint committee would vote in the bill's favor and thereby recommend that the House and Senate accept it.

As the meeting proceeded, several of the Democrats reported that they had received thousands of letters and telephone calls from voters requesting favorable action. Their remarks indicated that all the Democrats were in favor of 1022. The Republicans, however, remained silent during the entire discussion. Representative Feron was puzzled. He had heard of no great opposition within the ranks of the Republican members of the committee, but something was obviously on their minds. It made him realize that a joint favorable might in the end depend very much on the vote of the committee's Democratic members. They numbered fifteen to the Republicans' eleven when everyone was present. There weren't many Democratic votes to spare, especially if a few of the party's members were absent when the vote came.

Representative Feron had hoped for a vote that day, but his hopes were suddenly dashed by a fellow Democrat, a senator who had often spoken in favor of the bill. The senator, a powerful figure in the Democratic party, moved that 1022 be *tabled* for a week. This was a parliamentary move to delay further discussion and a vote until then. The motion was seconded, and the chairman waited a moment for possible discussion. Representative Feron was about to speak, but the senator who had made the motion shook his head slightly to indicate that the motion should not be opposed or questioned. It was voted upon favorably, and a recess was called.

Outside the meeting room the senator took Representative Feron aside and said: "I am sorry about it happening that way, Mr. Feron, but I was caught by our majority leaders just before going in to the committee meeting. They said something very important had suddenly come up on your bill. Before a committee vote they want the matter discussed in caucus. They want us there at half past twelve in Room 519. They would have told you before the meeting, but they couldn't get to you."

At the caucus the Democratic members of two joint committees were present: the Committee on Public Health and Safety and the Committee on Roads and Bridges. The majority leaders of both the House and Senate and their assistants were in the room, as well as the Democratic state chairman. The last opened the meeting with an involved explanation of why it had been called. There was a serious and unavoidable problem for some of the Democrats on the Roads and Bridges Committee.

It was over a bill to provide $150 million for a new expressway, Route 12, along the western

fringes of the state. The highway had been prom-
ised by the governor, a Democrat, in his last election campaign, and he wanted to keep the promise.
He had put the $150 million in his proposed budget
and was asking the General Assembly to approve it.
But then a powerful citizens' group on the eastern
side of the state had begun pushing for a new
superhighway there. It would cost some $300 mil-
lion. The governor wasn't opposed to the highway,
but he didn't want it approved at this session. His

budget could not stand the expense for at least two more years. The governor had therefore asked the Democratic state chairman to see if the eastern highway might not be voted down, while at the same time approving the Route 12 money.

"Voting down the $300 million isn't too much of a problem," said the Democratic state chairman, biting his cigar, "but we have a really tough problem when it comes to voting the $150 million for Route 12.

"We've got six Democrats on Roads and Bridges all from the eastern side of the state, and, boy, they are catching it from the voters. That citizens' group out there wants their road, and if they catch our six Democrats voting for Route 12 but not for theirs, trouble will descend on us in the voting booths next fall."

"What has all this to do with the Committee on Public Health and Safety?" asked Representative Feron, anxious to learn why his bill had been tabled.

"Good question," answered the state chairman, "with a simple but very political answer. We need some Republican support on Route 12. Right now they are pretty solidly against it. But if we can be sure of just three of their votes in favor of Route 12, it will definitely go through. At the same time it will mean that our legislators from the eastern districts won't have to vote for it and incur the disfavor of their voters.

"Now the Republicans, I have just learned, want a favor in Public Health and Safety on your air-pollution bill. We may be able to do some horse trading for the votes we need on Route 12."

Representative Feron immediately realized why the Republicans had remained silent at the committee meeting that morning. Their state chairman had undoubtedly asked them to withhold their support from 1022 until the so-called horse trading had been discussed.

"I have had a talk with the Republican state chairman," said the Democratic party chief, "and he confirms what we suspected. They have received a great deal of pressure from businessmen on 1022. Specifically they want the time limit increased from two to five years on forcing pollution controls upon industry. Otherwise, they are really and truly in favor of 1022. Perhaps the change is worth it. Perhaps they have a point. At any rate, if it can be done, we can pick up the needed Republican support on Route 12."

Representative Feron was unhappy. It was horse

trading all right, and he wasn't opposed to such compromises when necessary. With all the public pressures put on legislators, such give-and-take is often the only way to get needed work done. But the representative who had coauthored 1022 was not sure that this particular trade was a wise one.

"How many voters are there in that highway group in the eastern districts?" he asked the state chairman.

"I don't know," said the chairman, "perhaps a few hundred, but they are making a lot of noise out there about people losing their tax money to the other side of the state. They are a wild bunch, and we should keep them off our backs this year. This is an election year. I can't let you forget that."

"It sure is election year," said Representative Feron, pulling some papers from his briefcase, "and in that respect let me give you a figure of interest." He looked at a piece of paper and then continued, "The Citizens Committee for Clean Air as of last week had 28,380 registered members."

The room was silent as the number settled into everyone's mind. Representative Feron looked at the chairman of the Roads and Bridges Committee, an important senator representing a large district in the middle of the state's biggest industrial city. "Do you know where the largest single group of that membership comes from?" asked the coauthor of Bill 1022.

"Well, I guess you don't need to tell me," said the senator. "Right back in my own home bailiwick."

"Correct," said the representative. "Nearly twelve thousand reside and vote in your home district."

"Does that mean in short that you don't intend to change your bill to help us on Route 12?" asked the state chairman abruptly.

"I haven't said," replied Representative Feron firmly. "But I hope everyone here thinks over your proposal very carefully. I get the feeling that someone is making a mistake about the seriousness of 1022. This is not just another highway. This is a matter of life and death for many, and people in this state want the air cleaned up fast. I am for that and intend to stick with it. So my answer about changing the time limit is in the negative. If someone else on Public Health and Safety wants to make the change I want them ready and willing also to take the responsibility publicly."

Everyone could feel the tension that followed this brief statement, for Representative Feron had just done something that most politicians ordinarily avoid. He was advising the state's political boss:

"Don't pick on my bill." Such an act could bring a politician close to political disaster because he might lose his party's support, but Representative Feron was obviously not concerned. He was popular in the small towns that formed his assembly district, and he did not depend on politics for a living. He could afford to be independent.

The state chairman rubbed his chin for most of a minute while the caucus uneasily waited for him to speak. When he finally replied, he did so with a smile spreading over his face.

"Mr. Feron," he said, "are you telling me to go elsewhere with my horse trading?"

Representative Feron returned the smile and said, "Well, I didn't mean to put it like that, but since you have phrased it in those terms . . . ."

The participants were generally relieved that the state chairman had the good judgment to change his mind in view of the statistics on membership of the Clean Air Citizens Committee. No one really wanted such a large and active group unhappy with his political party, especially the senator from the large industrial city.

"Okay," said the state chairman, "we will take our horse trading elsewhere. How about everybody doing some thinking on this? See if you can come up with an answer for Route 12. Meanwhile, I will give our Republican friends the word on 1022. No deal."

CHAPTER 8

Compromise and a Committee Vote

The following week the Public Health and Safety Committee untabled Bill 1022, and it was again brought up for discussion. The chairman once more offered Representative Feron the opportunity to speak first. This time he simply suggested two changes in the bill, which he had intended to propose the previous week. One would be to insert the exception requested by the firemen's training director, allowing permits to build open fires for teaching purposes. The other would authorize the proposed Clean Air Commission to establish a scholarship for students interested in air-pollution control. No one objected to the proposals, and the committee chairman asked that Representative Feron make the changes.

He then called for discussion, and it began with a Republican senator talking about the two-year time limit set by the bill for the establishment of air-pollution controls in industry. The senator admitted that his party's members had received considerable pressure to have the time limit extended to five years. He said that the greatest pressure came from the electrical power companies, where conversion to new fuels would be both time-consuming and expensive.

"Now I would like to make a proposal in behalf of all my Republican colleagues," said the senator. "We have looked very carefully into the request for extending the time from two to five years. Our conclusions may surprise you a little. We have decided that five years is really more time than these companies need. We have, however, also concluded that two years is too short, that it would impose an undue hardship. In fact, we feel that if the two-year limit is imposed on the companies the state's Public Service Commission may soon be forced to approve higher rates for electricity.

"Now what would be a fair limit? The other day we held a caucus and invited an engineer from the Public Service Commission to give us a frank opinion on this subject. He brought us a lot of data on the furnaces being used for power generation around the state, and he gave us a good idea of what it would mean to convert them. He was of the firm opinion that two years was too short, but he also felt that five was longer than necessary.

"If this committee wishes, the Public Service engineer will be glad to make the same presentation before us. We have, however, asked him to write a technical paper on the subject. I have enough copies here for all of us. It will take only a few minutes to read, and I think it explains his points pretty clearly. If you will read it, I would then like to propose a change in the bill."

The copies were passed around the table, and everyone read the material carefully. It was a convincing paper well supported with facts and statistics. It clearly proved that two years was an extremely short time for converting furnaces in the electrical-generating industry.

When everyone had finished reading, the Republican senator continued: "In light of this presentation, I would like to propose that we change the two-year limit to three years for all large industrial furnace installations. In addition we might offer an electrical company a chance to appeal to the Clean Air Commission for an extension beyond three years if the firm can really prove undue hardship."

"What do you think of that?" said the chairman of the Public Health and Safety Committee. He looked around at his Democratic colleagues, settling on Representative Feron. "Do you want to hear the engineer from the Public Service Commission?"

"Not necessarily," said Representative Feron. "Frankly I would like some time to think this over in private. I am impressed by the paper that our esteemed Republican colleague has presented. I think it has merit, but I want a chance to go over it a bit further. Could we take a short recess?"

A sixty-minute recess was granted, and the committee members left the room. Representative Feron was actually anxious to find Senator Baldwin and talk over the proposal. The representative had read the technical paper with considerable surprise. For weeks he had steadfastly clung to the two-year limit, having concluded that industry really didn't need the extension. He had jumped to that conclusion during the public hearings when the lobbyist had called for a five-year limit. Now he was suddenly convinced that there was a case for granting at least three years, as proposed by the Republican senator. In fact he felt it was a fair compromise that

might remove practically all Republican opposition to Bill 1022.

The representative hurriedly found his coauthor of 1022, and they sat on a bench in the Senate chamber while Senator Baldwin read the technical paper. He too agreed it was convincing. He also agreed that the compromise might ensure that 1022 would sail through the General Assembly with a tremendous vote of approval.

"Go back to the committee," said the senator, "and agree to the change. Meanwhile let me get onto the telephone. This has to be explained quickly to the chairman of the Citizens Committee for Clean Air. And I had better call our party headquarters and tell the state chairman what is up. We have had all these people supporting the two-year limit. Now we have to let them know why we've agreed to a change, or they'll think we have let them down."

Around noon that day Bill 1022 was voted out of the Public Health and Safety Committee with a joint favorable recommending that the measure be enacted by the Senate and House. The final approved version called for a three-year time limit for conversion of large industrial furnaces, and it gave the Clean Air Commission the authority to extend the time given to electrical generating companies if undue hardship could be proved. After the vote was taken and the committee meeting adjourned, there was considerable handshaking between the Democratic and Republican members. Little interparty discussion had occurred on 1022 prior to this meeting, and a feeling of tension had arisen over the bill between the legislators of opposing political views. Suddenly the source of the tension had been erased without any problems, and everyone felt good about it.

As Representative Feron left the capitol and

drove home that day, he realized that once more his service in the General Assembly had taught him something about himself and the workings of democracy. He recognized that prejudice concerning lobbyists had kept him from giving even a look at the other side of the time-limit question. From his first day as a representative in the General Assembly he had decided without much cause that he should distrust lobbyists because they always had an ax to grind. Since a lobbyist had been among the first to propose an extension in the time limit, Representative Feron had without thought automatically decided against it. But then in the committee that day a very reasonable man, the Republican senator, had spoken up, and Representative Feron had learned that he had been making a mistake. The experience of having his mind changed made him realize again that the democratic process works best when reasonable men of differing opinions can talk and listen to one another.

CHAPTER 9

Vote, Vote, Vote

Because the air-pollution measure had been changed in committee, it was returned briefly to the legislative commissioner to be checked again for correctness in form and wording. The bill was then forwarded to the House of Representatives where it received its second reading. This consisted of the clerk simply announcing that 1022 had been reported favorably from the Public Health and Safety Committee.

Since the bill called for the use of state funds, it was then assigned by the Speaker to the Appropriations Committee, which decides if the state budget, mostly proposed by the governor, can afford the amounts requested by legislation. The sum called for in 1022 was small compared to many appropriations, and the committee quickly approved the request.

The measure was again returned to the House where the members automatically voted to "table for the calendar." With this motion the clerk listed 1022 on his calendar which serves as a schedule determining when a bill comes up for a vote before the House. Ordinarily a measure remains no more than three days on the clerk's calendar, and then, by the rules of the House, it has to be voted upon. But another motion was suddenly made involving 1022, and it changed the normal scheduling of the bill. A representative who was a member of the Public Health and Safety Committee called out, "Mr. Speaker, I move this bill be made the order of the day for May 5 at 2 P.M."

The motion, put to a vote by the Speaker, was accepted. It meant that Bill 1022 would not be held to the three-day rule, but would be retained on the clerk's calendar for action on May 5, which was more than two weeks away.

By accepting the order-of-the-day motion, the House gave 1022 special treatment often accorded important bills of great public interest. It established an advance date and hour for the bill's consideration. This would allow legislators extra time to prepare for debate, and provide the public with a lengthy notice of when the legislation would be considered.

In the two weeks prior to May 5 the Citizens Committee for Clean Air worked harder than ever, even though its members had been assured that 1022 would pass the General Assembly. The Citizens Committee's purpose was now to help the bill receive the largest vote possible. A wide majority of yeas cast in its favor might increase the vigor with which the law would be used to control air pollution.

In its nearly two years of life the Citizens Committee for Clean Air had raised more than $150,000, and this was now put to work educating the public on Bill 1022. It was accomplished mainly through newspaper advertisements discussing the dangers of air pollution. The readers were urged to telephone or write to their senators and representatives in behalf of the measure.

Much to the committee's surprise a large advertisement favoring 1022 appeared on May 1 in many state newspapers under sponsorship of the Manufacturers Association. It explained that industry favored the air-pollution control measure. The text ended with the state's businessmen pledging their full cooperation in cleaning up the air.

On May 5 the capitol corridors were again crowded with supporters of air-pollution control, and this time it was like a reunion. In more than eighteen months the Citizens Committee for Clean Air had brought people together in a common cause from all over the state. In that time they had pressed for a solution to a complicated, serious problem through legislation. The results of their labors were to be found in the House of Representatives that afternoon and in the Senate a few days later.

By now Senator Baldwin and Representative Feron could predict that their bill would pass by large majorities in both the House and the Senate. They had surveyed the votes in their respective chambers. Nearly all the Democrats in the Senate and the House were planning to vote for 1022. And in both chambers the bill's coauthors found enough Republicans favoring the measure to give it at least 70 percent of the total votes.

Though the bill's passage was certain, the on-lookers would still be treated to a public discussion of air pollution. Of course a bill frequently arrives for a vote without its future being settled, and the debate may then be a deciding factor. But more often than not, its fate has already been decided by discussion in party caucuses and standing committees. Then the speechmaking prior to the vote is mainly an open demonstration of individual points of view. Here a legislator's utterance becomes a matter of public record, for his words are recorded faithfully by a stenographer who officially transcribes them as a permanent part of the record of the General Assembly's proceedings. Many representatives now wanted to speak in favor of controlling air pollution. Bill 1022 had become known as a very popular measure, and the legislators wanted to demonstrate verbally that they stood on the winning side.

Shortly after two in the afternoon the members of the House of Representatives were nearly all in their seats, and the galleries were filled with citizens. The House was called to order by the Speaker; he noted that a quorum was present, and asked the chaplain for an opening prayer. After this formality was completed, the Speaker requested that the calendar be read by the clerk of the House, who announced:

"Bill Number 1022! An act concerning the elimination of air pollution! Reported favorably from the Committee on Public Health and Safety!"

This was the third and final reading for Bill 1022 in the House. The measure was still not read aloud, but a copy in its final printed form was now on every representative's desk. It was time for the passage or rejection of 1022 by the state's largest legislative body.

As the clerk's reading of the calendar ended, a representative who served on the joint Public Health and Safety Committee was on his feet. "Mr. Speaker," he called out, "I move the acceptance of the committee's favorable report and the passage of the bill."

The Speaker acknowledged the motion and indicated it was time for discussion on Bill 1022. He turned to the Democratic side of the House and pointed at Representative Feron who was already on his feet, holding a small microphone attached to his desk. Each representative and the Speaker have microphones that amplify their voices over a common loudspeaker system.

Representative Feron briefly outlined Bill 1022

and its history. He thanked all the people who had directly contributed to the research and writing of the bill, and he commended the thousands of citizens who had publicly supported the legislation. He concluded by saying: "I now call on all my colleagues in the House to vote yea on the question before us."

The Speaker of the House pointed to the Republican side of the room where the minority leader had risen to address the gathering. He began by stressing that from the very beginning his party had been for air-pollution control.

"Republicans also survive on air," said the minority leader, injecting into the proceedings some humor, "though at times some of our good friends on the other side of the House may think differently."

After a brief burst of laughter, the Republican leader continued: "For a time we were not sure that Bill 1022 was a fair piece of legislation, but as you know, it was changed in committee, and our party is more satisfied. We still have points of disagreement, but not serious ones. We hope that when the Clean Air Commission goes to work, it will iron out the problems that we see. We feel, for example, that the commission should exercise the good judgment of not recommending the possible maximum fine of five thousand dollars a week, except for the most flagrant violations."

The minority leader ended his speech by calling on his Republican colleagues in the House to vote in favor of 1022. It was certainly a different plea from what might have been made had the time limit for imposing controls been kept at two years. In that event the Republicans in caucus had planned to try changing the bill by appealing for the House of Representatives as a whole to raise the two-year limit to three. They would have done so by making a motion to amend Bill 1022, and the House would have had to vote on the amendment before voting on the full bill. The Republicans believed that the amendment would have been adopted because a strong case could have been made in its favor. But of course the change was granted in committee, making the move for an amendment unnecessary.

For the next hour speeches about Bill 1022 came first from a Democrat and then a Republican. Although all the Democrats and most of the Republicans were favorable to the bill, a few Republicans echoed the misgivings voiced by their minority leader.

The last speech, however, was unfavorable. Strange as it seemed to the visitors in the galleries, the opposing address came from a Democrat. He was a veteran representative of twenty-years service in the General Assembly. In the last several sessions the aging legislator had become absorbed by a fear that law after law was taking away one freedom after another until none would remain. Of course he recognized this danger again in 1022, which in his opinion would curb the freedom to make smoke at any time and in any way desired. What this elderly representative had lost sight of was the necessity for people occasionally to give up judiciously some freedoms for the good of everyone. With more people, more machines, and the extra complications of twentieth-century living, total freedom for individuals in some areas of life can not always be maintained without harm or discomfort to the majority of people.

When the veteran representative began speaking, all the other legislators settled into their chairs, knowing what the theme would be and that it would be long-winded. For thirty minutes the man employed his old-fashioned ornate oratory, passionately denouncing Bill 1022 as a "dastardly curb upon the God-given freedoms to use one's property and the air around it as he sees fit." If air pollution is to be controlled, he argued, each citizen should be allowed to take upon himself the making of necessary changes in his furnace, car, or rubbish burner. In his peroration, which he had repeated in the House many times, the orator, shaking a long finger at everyone around him, warned that the General Assembly was once more cutting down the freedom of the citizens of the state.

When he sat down and his booming voice stopped roaring through the huge chamber, the silence was stunning. But in a moment it was broken as someone yelled, "Vote!" In a few seconds almost the entire House of Representatives was shouting, "Vote!" "Vote!" "Vote!"

The Speaker rapped his gavel, though not very vigorously, and slowly the room quieted down. He looked from one side of the auditorium to the other and made sure that no one else cared to speak.

"The question is on the acceptance of Bill 1022," said the Speaker in a highly dignified manner. "All those in favor . . ."

His words were lost in the swell of voices calling "Yea!" in unison from the House floor. The sound vibrated against the paneled walls and ceiling. The great volume of sound left no question that the vast majority had voted in favor of the bill.

"All those opposed . . ." said the Speaker.

About five or six voices scattered throughout the hall yelled "Nay!" One came from the elderly Democratic representative. Two or three came from the Republican side of the House, but other than that, it was difficult to decide on the source of the nays.

"Bill 1022 is passed!" announced the Speaker.

If the vote had been closer or if someone had wanted to know exactly who voted for and against the bill, a motion might have been made by a representative to have a roll call vote. If, according to the rules of the House, one third of the members

101

had then agreed, Bill 1022 would have been voted upon again. Instead of calling out yea or nay, each representative would have made his choice by snapping a special switch to the left or right at the back of his desk. His vote would then have been recorded electronically in two places: on a large electric scoreboard on the wall of the House, and on a sheet of paper in a machine beside the clerk. In both places the yea or nay would have been recorded opposite the legislator's name and assembly district. The clerk would have removed the paper from the machine and made it a permanent record of the vote.

With Bill 1022 favorably voted by the House, the clerk sent it immediately to the Senate where it was tabled for the calendar. Three days later it was passed by the Senate with a unanimous vote from all present. As in the House some favorable speeches preceded the vote, primarily for the record.

With 1022 voted favorably by both the House and Senate it was sent to the legislative commissioner who gave the measure a final reading and then had the bill "engrossed." This simply meant that he arranged for the legislation to be printed in fancy type on a high grade of paper which would serve as the original and permanent document of the law. The commissioner signed the engrossed bill, and in the next couple of days it was sent to be signed by the clerk of the Senate and the clerk of the House. Their signatures officially verified that the bill had passed the two chambers. Finally the engrossed document was delivered to the secretary of the state who in turn gave it to the governor.

Three days later, in a public ceremony with the press, members of the Clean-Air Task Force, and a number of other officials present, the governor signed Bill 1022. It became a law that, according to the measure itself, would take effect ninety days from

the signing. If for some reason the governor had chosen not to sign the bill, it could have automatically become law after five days without his name. If however he had wanted to *veto,* that is reject the bill, he could have done so within the five days. He would then have had to return it to the General Assembly, unsigned but accompanied by a written reason for the rejection. But then the Senate and House could have voted again, and if two thirds of the members had voted yea, the bill would still have become law.

With the governor's signature affixed to the new air-pollution control law, it was returned to the secretary of the state who filed the original document and then made sure that copies were distributed, so that the text would be widely available to people. Now the state's highest officials had a law, a powerful tool, for cleaning up the air so crucial to all forms of life.

In the future the law would be applied by the governor through his *executive branch* of the state government. When people didn't obey the law, or when they felt it was unfair, the governor, or any private citizen involved, could turn to the state courts, the *judicial branch,* and ask the judges for settlement of the problems.

But the officials in both these branches would always remember that the law came from the *legislative branch,* which, of the three, is most clearly the people's branch. Through this branch the voters can give or refuse power to their rulers. This is why it is said that government in a democracy is government *by the people.*

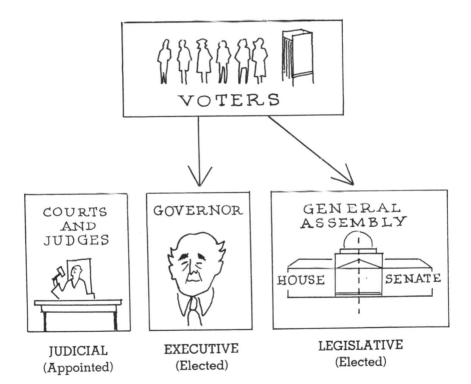

Index

air pollution, 1-7, 10-13, 15-17
  careers in field of, 65, 83
  control, 9, 20-22, 37-38, 60, 61-62, 84-89, 96, 98
  defined, 36-37
  family costs of, 19
  volume of, 18
assembly districts, 11
automobiles, 2, 16, 18
  exhaust controls on, 9, 21, 38

Clean Air, Citizens Committee for, 5-6, 8, 10, 88
  campaign of, 47, 55-56, 57, 61, 63, 93-94
  membership, 78-79, 81
  political parties and, 28-30, 31, 50, 51
Clean-Air Commission, 21, 37, 62, 98
  scholarships and, 65, 83
  time limits and, 85-86, 88

Clean-Air Task Force, 10-13, 103
  committee work of, 15-17
  report of, 17-23, 25, 26, 63
constitutionality, 34-35
costs, 16, 18-20
  of control, 9, 21-22, 38
  of education, 5-6, 93

Democratic party, 7, 94
  caucuses, 48-49, 50, 74-81
  central committee of, 26-32, 33
  General Assembly sessions and, 42, 44, 96-97, 99, 101
  joint committee sessions and, 73, 84, 86-89
  vote trading in, 76-78, 79-81

executive branch, 104

General Assembly, 3-4, 16, 41-52

General Assembly (*cont.*)
  bill introduction in, 7-9,
    25-26, 33, 36-37, 46-47,
    53-55
  bill passage in, 88, 91-105
  chambers of, 10-12
  committee work in, 47-52,
    54-55, 69-79, 87, 89, 95,
    99
  debate in, 95, 98-99
  highway appropriations of,
    75-76
  party interaction in, 32, 48-
    49, 96-99
  public hearings of, 57-67,
    71
governor, 4-5, 89
  Assembly sessions and, 45-
    46
  bill signature by, 103-104
  committee appointments
    by, 10, 12-13, 37
  highway appropriations
    and, 75-76
  industrial appeals to, 21-22
  lieutenant governor and,
    43
  reports to, 17-18, 20
  veto power of, 104

health, 1-2, 4, 5, 6, 16, 19-20,
    29, 36, 46, 66
  legislative committees on,
    49-51
heating, 16, 18, 21, 34
  conversion time limits, 65,
    77, 79, 84-89

House of Representatives
    (state), 3, 4, 10-11, 72,
    73, 91-92
  bills in, 7, 12, 32, 36, 48,
    53-54, 94-102, 103
  Speaker, 43, 44, 48, 52, 53-
    54, 92, 95, 96, 97, 101

incinerators, 2, 16, 18, 34, 62
  firefighter training and, 64,
    83
  industrial, 35-36
  municipal, 38
industry, 2, 16, 35-37
  conversion costs to, 9, 21-
    22, 38
  conversion time limits on,
    65, 77, 79, 84-89, 98
  labor vote and, 30, 31
  self-policing by, 59, 60, 62,
    63, 94
  violation fines on, 21, 38,
    61-62, 98

joint committees, 48
  caucuses, 74-81
  executive sessions, 71-73,
    83-89
judicial branch, 104

labor, 30, 31
legislative branch, 104
legislative commissioner, 8-
    9, 10, 33, 91, 102-103
Legislative Council, 25-26
legislature. *See* General As-
    sembly

108

lieutenant governor, 43-44, 45

lobbying, 42, 58, 59-62, 89

Motor Vehicle Commission, 38

press, 4, 6-7, 18, 41, 66, 103
  political advertising in, 93-94
Public Health and Safety, Committee on, 49, 50, 51, 54-56, 90, 94
  private sessions, 71-81, 83-89
  public hearings, 57-67, 71

Republican party, 31-32, 93
  caucuses, 49, 76-77
  central committee, 27
  General Assembly sessions and, 42, 44, 97-98, 101
  joint committee sessions and, 73, 84-87, 88, 89
  vote trading, 76-78, 79-81

Roads and Bridges, Committee on, 74-81

Senate (state), 3, 4, 11-12, 52, 53, 54
  bill passage in, 7, 12, 32, 36, 48, 94, 102, 103
  General Assembly joint session and, 42-43, 44-45, 47
  joint committee sessions and, 72, 74, 84, 87
senatorial districts, 11-12
standing committees, 47-48
State Health Department, 2, 20, 58
  problem study, 4-5, 6, 8, 17, 63
State Manufacturers Association, 21-22, 58, 94

Truman, Harry, quoted, 70

United States Constitution, 34

About the Author

Leonard Stevens was born in Lisbon, New Hampshire. He studied journalism and speech in college, and took his master's degree from the State University of Iowa.

Before he became a writer, Mr. Stevens worked as a member of a ski patrol and as a radio news editor. During World War II, he served as a captain in the United States Air Force.

Mr. Stevens has been interested and active in both state and local politics for many years. He is chairman of the Democratic Town Committee of his hometown. This book grew out of a study he did of the legislature in his own state.

In addition to numerous magazine articles, Leonard Stevens has written eight books on various subjects.

The author and his wife and their four children make their home in Bridgewater, Connecticut.

About the Illustrator

Robert Galster has illustrated many books, designed book jackets and record-album covers, and painted murals. He is also well known for his Broadway-theater poster designs.

Mr. Galster was born in Illinois, grew up in Ohio, and now makes his home in New York City.

DATE DUE

NOV 27			